The Excel for Beginners Quiz Book

M.L. HUMPHREY

TITLES BY M.L. HUMPHREY

EXCEL ESSENTIALS
Excel for Beginners
Intermediate Excel
50 Useful Excel Functions
50 More Excel Functions

EXCEL ESSENTIALS QUIZ BOOKS
The Excel for Beginners Quiz Book
The Intermediate Excel Quiz Book
The 50 Useful Excel Functions Quiz Book
The 50 More Excel Functions Quiz Book

DATA PRINCIPLES
Data Principles for Beginners

EASY EXCEL ESSENTIALS
Pivot Tables
Conditional Formatting
Charts
The IF Functions
Formatting
Printing

WORD ESSENTIALS
Word for Beginners
Intermediate Word

MAIL MERGE
Mail Merge for Beginners

POWERPOINT ESSENTIALS
PowerPoint for Beginners

BUDGETING FOR BEGINNERS
Budgeting for Beginners
Excel for Budgeting

.

CONTENTS

INTRODUCTION

This is a companion book written to complement *Excel for Beginners* by M.L. Humphrey and is geared towards those who are already familiar with the content covered in that book who now want to test their knowledge through quizzes or to those who learn better from a question and answer format.

For each chapter in *Excel for Beginners* there is a set of questions meant to test your knowledge of the information that was covered in the chapter.

The first section of the book just has the questions, the next section of the book has the questions as well as the answers. There is also a bonus section that contains five exercises where you can test your knowledge of the various functions by applying them to specific real-life scenarios.

I encourage you to try to do each exercise first without looking at the solutions, since in the real world you'll be faced with a problem that needs solved and no one will be there to tell you how to solve it. However, I would also encourage you to have Excel open as you work each exercise so you can use the help functions within Excel to find what you need. Don't feel like you need to memorize every task in Excel in order to use it effectively. You just need to know what's possible and then what keywords or phrasing to use to help you find the information that will let you perform the right task.

Alright, then. Let's start with the first quiz.

QUIZZES

TERMINOLOGY QUIZ

1. In an Excel worksheet what are generally identified by letters that run across the top of the worksheet?
    a. Columns
    b. Rows
    c. Cells
    d. Other

2. In an Excel worksheet what are generally identified by numbers that run along the left-hand side of the worksheet?
    a. Columns
    b. Rows
    c. Cells
    d. Other

3. What is a cell?

4. How do you know what cell or cell(s) you have selected?

5. In general, what does left-clicking do?

6. In general, what does right-clicking do?

7. What is the difference between a worksheet and a workbook in Excel?

8. What is the formula bar?

9. What is a scroll bar?

10. How can you use a scroll bar?
    a. Click on the bar and drag.
    b. Click on the space to either side of the bar.
    c. Click on the arrows at the top and bottom or on each end of the scroll bar space.
    d. All of the above.

11. With a scroll bar if you want to move outside of the area where you've already entered information, which method should you use?

12. Name two ways that you can select cells in a worksheet.

13. What is a dropdown menu?

14. What is a dialogue box?

15. How can you access a dialogue box?

ABSOLUTE BASICS QUIZ

1. What is the Ctrl shortcut you can use to save a file?

2. Which of the following methods works to open an existing Excel file:

> a. Double-click on the file name where it's stored on your computer

> b. Open Excel and choose the file name from the list under Recent on the left-hand side or navigate to the file location by clicking on Open Other Workbooks at the bottom of the page.

> c. If you're already in Excel, go to File and then choose Open from the left-hand side menu and then choose a file name from under Recent Workbooks or navigate to the file you want using the Computer option.

> d. All of the above.

3. What is the difference between Save and Save As?

4. Discuss why you might save a file as an .xls file type instead of an .xlsx file type.

5. Name three ways to save a file.

6. How can you delete an existing Excel file?

7. How can you rename an existing Excel file?

8. What issue should you be aware of if you move or rename an Excel file that you recently used?

NAVIGATING EXCEL QUIZ

1. When you open a new Excel file, what cell and worksheet does it open to?

2. When you open an existing Excel file, what cell and worksheet does it open to?

3. Name two ways you could use to get to Cell B6 if you were in Cell A1?

4. What does the Shift key do? What does Shift + Tab do?

5. In a worksheet that has a lot of data in it, what is a quick way to scroll down a large number of rows or to scroll over a large number of columns?

6. What is one very important thing you need to remember when using scrollbars to navigate an Excel worksheet?

7. Name two ways to move to a different worksheet than the one you're currently in.

8. What does using the F2 key do?

9. Name two ways to insert a cell into a worksheet.

10. What do the different insert cell options (shift cells right, shift cells down, entire row, and entire column) do?

11. Name three ways you can insert a row or column into a worksheet.

12. How do you select an entire row or column?

13. How do you insert a new worksheet into an Excel workbook?

14. How do you delete a cell in a worksheet?

15. What is the problem you might run into when you either insert a cell or cells or delete a cell or cells from a worksheet that has existing data?

16. How do you delete a column or row?

17. How do you delete a worksheet?

18. How do you rename a worksheet?

INPUTTING YOUR DATA QUIZ

1. What is the most basic way to input data in a cell in an Excel worksheet?

2. Which of the following are bad ways of inputting data in an Excel worksheet?

    a. Not labeling each column of your data.

    b. Breaking up your data entries with summary entries.

    c. Allowing users to enter data in any way and any format they want.

    d. Using a lot of free text entry fields.

    e. All of the above.

3. What is a best practice when handling a data set that you need to analyze?

4. What does Ctrl + Z do?

5. What does Ctrl + Y do?

6. If you have to make a large number of entries in a column in Excel that have a limited number of values (say, book, CD, and video), what's an easy trick for entering that information that will save you a lot of time?

7. Does auto-suggested text work with numbers?

8. Name two ways to copy the contents of a cell.

9. Name two ways to cut the contents of a cell from its current location.

10. Name two ways to paste the contents of a cell into a new location.

11. When it comes to formulas, what is the difference between Copying the contents of a cell and Cutting the contents of a cell?

12. What does using the $ sign in a formula do?

13. What does Paste Special – Values do?

14. What does Paste Special – Transpose do?

15. How can you display the contents of a cell as text without Excel trying to convert it into a date or formula?

16. How do you tell Excel that you're entering a formula into a cell?

17. How can you include line breaks within a cell in Excel (since hitting enter will just take you to the next cell)?

18. How can you delete data you've entered into a cell without deleting the cell?

19. What does Find do?

20. What does Replace do?

21. What is the danger of using Replace?

22. How do you access Find and Replace?

23. If you want to have a list of 250 entries that repeat the days of the week (Monday, Tuesday, Wednesday, etc.) what is the easiest way to do that?

24. What does Freeze Panes do?

25. How do you Freeze Panes?

26. What is one thing to be careful of when using Freeze Panes?

FORMATTING QUIZ

1. What are the Ctrl shortcuts for bolding, italics, and underlining?

2. What are the six basic cell alignment choices you have available to you?

3. How do you align text within a cell?

4. If you want to change the angle of text, how do you do that?

5. What are two other ways to bold text other than using a Ctrl shortcut?

6. What are two other ways to italicize text other than using a Ctrl shortcut?

7. What are two other ways to underline text other than using a Ctrl shortcut?

8. If you have selected text that is partially formatted in bold, italic, or underline and partially not, what will happen

when you click on the B, I, or U for bold, italic, or underline formatting?

9. When should you choose the style of border that you want to use for a given cell?

10. How can you put a diagonal border line through a cell?

11. Name two ways to apply a standard border to a cell.

12. If you just want a simple border around all of your cells, what's the best border option to use?

13. To put a darker perimeter border around a range of cells, what default option can you choose?

14. How do you clear all borders from around a cell or cells?

15. How do you add background color to a cell?

16. If you need to use a custom fill color or custom font color, how do you do this?

17. Name three ways to adjust the width of a column.

18. How can you adjust all of your column widths at once?

19. How do you select all cells in a worksheet?

20. Name three ways to adjust the height of a row.

21. How can you adjust all of your row heights at once?

22. How do you get text to wrap to the next line?

23. Name three ways you can apply currency formatting to a cell or range of cells.

24. Name two ways you can apply date formatting to a cell or range of cells.

25. What is one thing to be careful of when using dates in Excel?

26. Name two ways you can change the font used in a cell or range of cells.

27. Name four ways to change the size of the font used in a cell or range of cells.

28. How do you change the color of the text in a cell or range of cells?

29. If you've placed a dark fill color into a cell, what font color might you want to use?

30. What does Merge & Center do?

31. When might you want to use Merge & Center?

32. How do you Merge & Center a range of cells?

33. If you want to format a range of cells as a number with four decimal places, how would you do that?

34. How do you format a number as a percentage?

35. If you have the number .10 what is that as a percentage?

36. What does the Format Painter allow you to do?

37. How do you use the Format Painter?

38. What would happen if you click on the Format Painter tool and then try to use the arrow keys to navigate to the

cell where you want to apply that formatting?

39. How can you apply formatting to multiple cells that are not touching without having to go through the whole Format Painter process each time?

MANIPULATING YOUR DATA QUIZ

1. What does Sorting do?

2. Do you need to have a header row to sort data?

3. If your data does have a header row, what do you need to make sure you do when you are telling Excel how to sort your data?

4. What will happen if your data has a header row but Excel doesn't know that?

5. Should you include a summary row in your sort?

6. Name three ways to sort a range of data.

7. If the sort options that you see are Column A, Column B, Column C, etc. what does this mean?

8. What order should you list your sort criteria in?

9. If you want to sort text in an alphabetical order, which sort options should you choose?

10. If you want to sort numbers from largest to smallest, which sort options should you choose?

11. If you have a range that contains days of the week or months of the year, what sort options should you choose?

12. If you added a sort level that you don't need, how do you remove it?

13. How do you change the order in which your data will be sorted when you have multiple sort criteria listed?

14. What are some issues to be aware of when sorting?

15. What should you do if you sort data and realize you made a mistake?

16. What does filtering do?

17. How do you turn on filtering?

18. If you add a new column of data, will filtering extend to that new column?

19. How will you know when you have filtering turned on?

20. Once you've turned on filtering, how do you filter a specific column?

21. In recent versions of Excel, what options do you have for filtering data?

22. Using filtering, if you just want to see two or three specific entries in a column but have a large number of different values that are possible in that column, what's a quick trick to do that?

23. Using filtering, if you want to see all of the entries that contain the word "USA", how would you do that?

24. Using filtering, if you want to see all of the entries that have red text, how would you do that?

25. Using filtering, if you want to see all of the entries with a numerical value greater than 100, how would you do that?

26. How can you tell when your worksheet values have already been filtered?

27. How can you tell which columns have filtering in place?

28. How do you remove filtering from a specific column?

29. How do you remove filtering from all columns in a worksheet?

30. How do you turn off filtering?

31. How do you tell Excel that you want to use a function?

32. What is the function you can use to sum a range of values?

33. What is the function you can use to multiply a range of values?

34. Is there a function for subtracting values?

35. Is there a function for dividing values?

36. What is the symbol you can use to add two values?

37. What is the symbol you can use to multiply two values?

38. What is the symbol you can use to subtract two values?

39. What is the symbol you can use to divide two values?

40. What cells am I referencing if I write =SUM(A1:B3)?

41. What cells am I referencing if I write =SUM(A1,B3)?

42. What cells am I referencing if I write =SUM(A:B)?

43. What cells am I referencing if I write =SUM(1:3)?

44. If you just want to know what the sum of a range of cells is but don't need to record that value anywhere, what is one option you have for seeing that sum?

45. How can you see what cells are being used in a formula?

46. What does AutoSum do?

47. Where can you find the AutoSum option?

48. What is one thing to be careful about when using AutoSum?

49. If you want to subtract the values in Cells B1, C1, and D1 from the value in Cell A1, what's the best way to do that?

50. How can you get Excel to help you write your formulas?

51. Is it possible to use Excel to conduct complex calculations in one cell?

52. How do you find a function that can do what you want to do?

53. What does it mean that formulas in Excel are relative?

54. Why is it good that formulas in Excel are relative?

55. What if you want to keep a reference fixed when you copy a formula? For example, Cell A1 includes the unit price and you want that fixed no matter where you copy the formula to?

56. What if you just want to move a formula but you don't want any of the cell references to change. How would you do that?

PRINTING QUIZ

1. What is the control shortcut for printing?

2. How else can you access the print option?

3. If you're ready to print and don't need to make any changes, what button do you click on to print?

4. If you want to print on both sides of the page, which option should you change?

5. When is it best to use print on both sides long-edge versus print on both sides short-edge?

6. What does it mean to print a document collated versus uncollated?

7. What does Print Selection do?

8. What does Print Active Sheets do?

9. What does Print Entire Workbook do?

10. What does Print Selected Pages do?

11. How do you change the printer you're using to print?

12. How do you specify the number of copies to print?

13. What is the difference between portrait orientation and landscape orientation?

14. How do you choose what type of paper to print on?

15. What should you be careful about when selecting the type of paper to print on?

16. What does the margins setting let you do?

17. What does scaling let you do?

18. What should you be careful about when using page scaling?

19. What's one trick for working with scaling if the data isn't going to fit well on the page?

20. Where can you go to scale your document?

21. Where can you go to center your print output horizontally and/or vertically on the page?

22. What does setting a Print Area on a document do?

23. When is setting the Print Area useful?

24. What are the dangers of using Print Area?

25. What's the best way to set the Print Area?

26. What does Print Titles allow you to do?

27. How do you set Print Titles?

28. What should you be careful of when using Print Titles?

CONCLUSION QUIZ

1. Name three ways to find more information if you get stuck.

2. What else can you do if you get stuck?

QUIZ ANSWERS

TERMINOLOGY QUIZ ANSWERS

1. In an Excel worksheet what are generally identified by letters that run across the top of the worksheet?
a. Columns

2. In an Excel worksheet what are generally identified by numbers that run along the left-hand side of the worksheet?
b. Rows

3. What is a cell?
A combination of a row and column that is identified by the letter of the column it's in and the number of the row it's in.

4. How do you know what cell or cell(s) you have selected?
The cell or cells will have a darker border around them. When you've selected cells that are not touching the most recently selected cell will be surrounded by a darker border and the other cells will be shaded in gray.

5. In general, what does left-clicking do?

It selects the item.

6. In general, what does right-clicking do?

It shows a dropdown list of options to choose from.

7. What is the difference between a worksheet and a workbook in Excel?

A worksheet is just one tab that contains a combination of rows and columns within an Excel workbook. A workbook is an entire Excel file. There can be more than one worksheet in an Excel workbook. Worksheets are initially labeled Sheet1, Sheet2, etc.

8. What is the formula bar?

The formula bar is the bar at the top of the screen when you're in Excel with the fx symbol next to it. If you start to type text into a cell, the formula bar will also show what you type. If you input a formula into a cell and then hit enter and go back to that cell, the value returned by the formula will show in the cell, while the formula bar will show the formula being used.

9. What is a scroll bar?

A scroll bar is a bar at the side or bottom of the screen that you can use to navigate through an Excel worksheet.

10. How can you use a scroll bar?

d. All of the above. (Click on the bar and drag, click on the space to either side of the bar, and click on the arrows at the top and bottom or on each end of the scroll bar space.)

11. With a scroll bar if you want to move outside of the area where you've already entered information, which method should you use?

Use the arrows at the ends of the scroll bar.

12. Name two ways that you can select cells in a worksheet.

Left-click and drag your mouse to highlight cells that are touching. Or, left-click on the first cell, hold down the Ctrl key, and then left-click on any other cells you want to select.

13. What is a dropdown menu?

It's a list of potential choices that you can select from, generally indicated by the existence of a small arrow next to the visible choice for that item. See, for example, the list of fonts under the Font section of the Home tab.

14. What is a dialogue box?

It's a pop-up menu of choices for a given task. Generally, dialogue boxes will contain the most choices for a task whereas the information in the tabs contains the most frequently used options.

15. How can you access a dialogue box?

Often they are available when you see a small arrow in the bottom right corner of a section of a tab. See, for example, the Font section of the Home tab.

ABSOLUTE BASICS QUIZ ANSWERS

1. What is the Ctrl shortcut you can use to save a file?
Ctrl + S

2. Which of the following methods works to open an existing Excel file:
d. All of the above. (Double-click on the file name where it's stored on your computer, open Excel and choose the file name from the list under Recent on the left-hand side or navigate to the file location by clicking on Open Other Workbooks at the bottom of the page, or if you're already in Excel, go to File and then choose Open from the left-hand side menu and then choose a file name from under Recent Workbooks or navigate to the file you want using the Computer option.)

3. What is the difference between Save and Save As?
Save will save the file using its existing name, location, and file type and will overwrite the prior version of the file. Save As allows you to change the file name, location, or file type and, if you do so, will not overwrite the prior version of the file. For new files, Excel always defaults to Save As.

4. Discuss why you might save a file as an .xls file type instead of an .xlsx file type.

An .xls file type should be one that anyone with any version of Excel can open. With an .xlsx file type only those who have Excel 2007 or later can open it. So if you're going to share the file and aren't sure what version of Excel the other person is working with, it's better to use the .xls file type, assuming you haven't used any functions that weren't available in prior versions of Excel.

5. Name three ways to save a file.

Ctrl + S, File>Save, click on the image of a computer disk in the top left corner of your screen.

6. How can you delete an existing Excel file?

By navigating to where you have the file saved and deleting it from there. You can either click on the file and then choose Delete from the menu at the top of the box or you can right-click and choose Delete from the dropdown menu.

7. How can you rename an existing Excel file?

You can either choose to Save As and rename the file that way but it will leave you with two versions of the file, one under the old name, one under the new name. Or you can navigate to where the file is saved, click on the file name once to select it, once more to highlight the name, and then type in your new name there.

8. What issue should you be aware of if you move or rename an Excel file that you recently used?

You won't be able to open the file from the list of Recent Workbooks in Excel since the file was moved or renamed and the path that Excel has for it is no longer accurate. You will either need to go to where the file is stored and open it from there or navigate to the file using the Computer option under Open.

NAVIGATING EXCEL QUIZ ANSWERS

1. When you open a new Excel file, what cell and worksheet does it open to?

Cell A1 of Sheet1.

2. When you open an existing Excel file, what cell and worksheet does it open to?

Wherever you were when you last saved the file. This means that it may open with a set of cells already selected.

3. Name two ways you could use to get to Cell B6 if you were in Cell A1?

Left-click on Cell B6. Use the arrow keys to navigate from Cell A1 to Cell B6.

4. What does the Shift key do? What does Shift + Tab do?

The shift key lets you move one cell to the right. Using shift + tab lets you move one cell to the left.

5. In a worksheet that has a lot of data in it, what is a quick way to scroll down a large number of rows or to scroll over a large number of columns?

Click and hold the scroll bar as you drag it either down or over.

6. What is one very important thing you need to remember when using scrollbars to navigate an Excel worksheet?

Until you click into a new cell in the worksheet you will still be in the last cell you clicked on or edited. This means you can scroll down thousands of rows in a worksheet, but if you forget to click into one of the now-visible cells, when you use your arrow key or start typing you will be doing so in the cell thousands of rows away from where you scrolled to.

7. Name two ways to move to a different worksheet than the one you're currently in.

Left-click on the name of the worksheet you want to move to. Or use Ctrl + Page Up to move one worksheet to the left or Ctrl + Page Dn to move one worksheet at a time to the right. (If you're on a computer where the arrow keys and the Page Up/Page Dn keys have been combined you may actually need to use Ctrl + Fn + Page Up and Ctrl + Fn +Page Dn.)

8. What does using the F2 key do?

It takes you to the end of the contents of the current cell. It can be very useful when you need to edit the contents of a cell and don't want to switch to using your mouse or trackpad.

9. Name two ways to insert a cell into a worksheet.

Click in the cell where you want to insert a cell and then right-click and choose Insert from the dropdown menu. Or click in the cell where you want to insert a cell and then go to the Cells section of the Home tab and choose Insert Cells from the Insert dropdown menu.

10. What do the different insert cell options (shift cells right, shift cells down, entire row, and entire column) do?

Shift cells right will insert a cell (or cells) by shifting the selected cell or cells to the right. Shift cells down will insert a cell (or cells) by shifting the selected cell or cells down. Entire row will insert one entire row for each row in the selected range of cells. Entire column will insert one entire column for each column in the selected range of cells.

11. Name three ways you can insert a row or column into a worksheet.

You can select a cell, right click, choose Insert, and then choose Entire Row to insert a row or Entire Column to insert a column. You can also highlight the entire row or column, right-click, and select Insert. Or you can highlight the row or column and then go to the Cells section of the Home tab and choose the option you want from the Insert dropdown menu.

12. How do you select an entire row or column?

Click on the letter of the column or the number of the row.

13. How do you insert a new worksheet into an Excel workbook?

Click on + symbol in a circle (or in older versions of Excel the mini worksheet with a yellow star in the corner) that is at the end of the list of your existing worksheets. Or go to the Home tab and under the Cells section and choose Insert Sheet from the Insert dropdown menu.

14. How do you delete a cell in a worksheet?

Right-click on the cell you want to delete and choose Delete from the dropdown menu. From there choose whether to shift cells up or left to replace the deleted cell. You can also select the cell and then go to the Cells section of the Home tab and click on the Delete dropdown menu and choose Delete Cells from there.

15. What is the problem you might run into when you either insert a cell or cells or delete a cell or cells from a worksheet that has existing data?

You can inadvertently change the alignment of your remaining data so that the data no longer matches up. To avoid this issue, you may sometimes need to insert or delete more cells to keep all of your existing data aligned.

16. How do you delete a column or row?

Highlight the entire column or row you want to delete, right-click, and choose Delete from the dropdown menu. Or you can highlight the column or row, go to the Cells section of the Home tab, and choose the option from the Delete dropdown menu.

17. How do you delete a worksheet?

Right-click on the worksheet name and choose Delete. You can also go to the Cells section of the Home tab and use the Delete Sheet option from the Delete dropdown menu.

18. How do you rename a worksheet?

Double left-click on the worksheet name and then delete the existing name and replace it with the name you want. You can also right-click on the worksheet name and choose Rename from the dropdown menu.

INPUTTING YOUR DATA
QUIZ ANSWERS

1. What is the most basic way to input data in a cell in an Excel worksheet?

Click and start typing.

2. Which of the following are bad ways of inputting data in an Excel worksheet?

e. All of the above. (Not labeling each column of your data, breaking up your data entries with summary entries, allowing users to enter data in any way and any format they want, using a lot of free text entry fields.)

3. What is a best practice when handling a data set that you need to analyze?

Store the raw data in one location, analyze and correct that data in a separate location.

4. What does Ctrl + Z do?

It undoes the last thing you did in Excel.

5. What does Ctrl + Y do?

It redoes the last thing you did in Excel.

6. If you have to make a large number of entries in a column in Excel that have a limited number of values (say, book, CD, and video), what's an easy trick for entering that information that will save you a lot of time?

You can use the Excel auto-suggested text feature to make your entries. As long as the entries all start with a different letter, you've already entered each one at least once, and your entries are continuous, when you type the first letter of each entry Excel will suggest to you that word that you already used and you can just hit enter to have Excel populate that cell with the entire word even though you only typed the first letter.

7. Does auto-suggested text work with numbers?

No. It only works with entries that have letters in them. It will work with something like 123alpha but only when you type 123a. Until then it won't work.

8. Name two ways to copy the contents of a cell.

Click on the cell and type Ctrl + C. Right-click on the cell and choose Copy from the dropdown menu. (You can also use the Copy option in the Clipboard section of the Home tab.)

9. Name two ways to cut the contents of a cell from its current location.

Click on the cell and type Ctrl + X. Right-click on the cell and choose Cut from the dropdown menu. (You can also use the Cut option in the Clipboard section of the Home tab.)

10. Name two ways to paste the contents of a cell into a new location.

After you've copied or cut the contents of a cell, you can go to the new location, click into the cell where you want the information and hit enter. You can also use Ctrl

+ V at the new location. The advantage of using Ctrl + V is that it allows you to paste those values into more than one location as long as the information was copied not cut from its prior location. (You can also use the Paste option in the Clipboard section of the Home tab.)

11. When it comes to formulas, what is the difference between Copying the contents of a cell and Cutting the contents of a cell?

If you Cut the contents of a cell and place them in a new location, the formula remains exactly the same as it was. So =A1+B1 will still be =A1+B1. If you Copy the contents of a cell and place them in a new location, the formula will adjust relative to its new location. So if you move a formula that was =A1+B1 down two rows it will become =A3+B3. If you move it over two columns instead it will become =C1+D1.

12. What does using the $ sign in a formula do?

It fixes the row or column reference so that if the formula is copied to another cell, the row or column reference will stay the same. For example, if the formula was =$A1+B$1, meaning keep the Column A reference in A1 fixed and the Row 1 reference in B1 fixed, then if that formula is copied down two rows, the formula would now be =$A3+B$1. And if it was copied over two columns instead it would be =$A1+D$1. Using the dollar sign for both the row and column, so for example A1, means that the reference to that particular cell will remain the same no matter where the formula is copied.

13. What does Paste Special – Values do?

It allows you to paste copied entries and only retain the values of any calculations from the copied cells without also copying the formulas or formatting. This also lets you paste in values but use the formatting of the destination cells instead of the originating cells.

14. What does Paste Special – Transpose do?

It allows you to copy a row of values and paste them as a column of values or to copy a column of values and paste them as a row. Be careful with this one that you don't overwrite existing data.

15. How can you display the contents of a cell as text without Excel trying to convert it into a date or formula?

Use a single quotation mark to start your entry. For example '-Item A will display as –Item A but not using the single quotation mark will have Excel trying to treat that as a formula.

16. How do you tell Excel that you're entering a formula into a cell?

By starting the entry with a -, +, or = sign. It's best to use the = sign if you can.

17. How can you include line breaks within a cell in Excel (since hitting enter will just take you to the next cell)?

By using Alt + Enter.

18. How can you delete data you've entered into a cell without deleting the cell?

Click in the cell and use your delete key to remove the contents. You can also use F2 or double-click to get into the cell and then use the backspace key. To delete the contents of a cell as well as the formatting on the cell, go to the Editing section of the Home tab and choose Clear All from the Clear dropdown menu.

19. What does Find do?

It allows you to find an entry that matches your criteria.

20. What does Replace do?

It allows you to find an entry that matches your criteria and replace it with another value.

21. What is the danger of using Replace?

If you're not careful in specifying what you wanted to find, you can end up replacing part of an entry you didn't intend to replace. For example, if you try to replace "hat" with "chapeau" and are not specific that you're only looking for the full word hat, you can end up replacing all occurrences of hat with chapeau even if they are part of words like that and chat.

22. How do you access Find and Replace?

To access Find and Replace you can use Ctrl +F or Ctrl + H to bring up the Find and Replace dialogue box. There's one tab for each option. Or you can go to the Editing section of the Home tab, click on Find & Select and then choose Find or Replace from the dropdown menu there.

23. If you want to have a list of 250 entries that repeat the days of the week (Monday, Tuesday, Wednesday, etc.) what is the easiest way to do that?

Start with Monday in the first cell and then left-click in the bottom right corner and drag until you have the number of entries you want. Excel should auto-complete the rest of the entries Monday, Tuesday, Wednesday, Thursday, Friday, Saturday, Sunday, Monday, etc. (If that doesn't work, fill in the first four cells or so and then try it.)

24. What does Freeze Panes do?

It allows you to specify rows at the top of the worksheet and/or columns at the left-hand side of the worksheet that you want to keep always visible.

25. How do you Freeze Panes?

Go to the View tab and choose Freeze Panes from the

Window section. From there choose whether you want to Freeze Top Row, Freeze First Column, or Freeze Panes. Freeze Panes will freeze all of the columns to the left of the cell you're clicked into and all of the rows above the cell you're clicked into.

26. What is one thing to be careful of when using Freeze Panes?

If you're clicked into one of the top rows or side columns that you've frozen and you arrow down or over to an area that isn't frozen you can lose your place, because arrowing down or over will take you to the next row or column not necessarily the rows or columns that are visible to you at that moment.

Also, if you freeze too many panes you won't be able to see any of your other data.

FORMATTING QUIZ ANSWERS

1. What are the Ctrl shortcuts for bolding, italics, and underlining?

Ctrl + B to bold, Ctrl + I to italicize, and Ctrl + U to underline.

2. What are the six basic cell alignment choices you have available to you?

Left, Center, Right, Top, Middle, Bottom

3. How do you align text within a cell?

Click on the cell, go to the Alignment section of the Home tab, and choose and click on the cell alignment option that you want to use. The images on the buttons show each alignment type. Another option is to right-click on the cell and choose Format Cells from the dropdown menu. From there go to the Alignment tab and change the Horizontal and Vertical dropdown options to what you want.

4. If you want to change the angle of text, how do you do that?

One option is to click on the cell and then go to the Alignment section of the Home tab and choose from one of the options under the Orientation dropdown (the ab with an angled arrow under it on the top row). Another option is to right-click, choose Format Cells from the dropdown menu, go to the Alignment tab, and then in the Orientation section on the right-hand side choose the degree to which you want to angle your text.

5. What are two other ways to bold text other than using a Ctrl shortcut?

Click on the large capital B in the Font section of the Home tab. Right-click, choose Format Cells from the dropdown menu, go to the Font tab, and choose Bold for your Font Style.

6. What are two other ways to italicize text other than using a Ctrl shortcut?

Click on the slanted capital I in the Font section of the Home tab. Right-click, choose Format Cells from the dropdown menu, go to the Font tab, and choose Italic for your Font Style.

7. What are two other ways to underline text other than using a Ctrl shortcut?

Click on the underlined capital U in the Font section of the Home tab. Right-click, choose Format Cells from the dropdown menu, go to the Font tab, and choose an option from the Underline dropdown menu.

8. If you have selected text that is partially formatted in bold, italic, or underline and partially not, what will happen when you click on the B, I, or U for bold, italic, or underline formatting?

It will apply that formatting to the entire selection. Which means to remove that type of formatting from a selection that is partially formatted that way you will need to click on the option twice, once to apply the formatting to the entire selection, once to remove it.

9. When should you choose the style of border that you want to use for a given cell?

Before you apply that border to that cell. If you don't, the border applied to the cell will be the default or current border format you have selected.

10. How can you put a diagonal border line through a cell?

Highlight the cell, right-click, choose Format Cells, go to the Border tab and click on the diagonal option in the bottom corner under the Border section.

11. Name two ways to apply a standard border to a cell.

Use the Border dropdown option in the Font section of the Home tab. Or right-click on the cell, choose Format Cells, go to the Border tab, and click on the border option there.

12. If you just want a simple border around all of your cells, what's the best border option to use?

All Borders.

13. To put a darker perimeter border around a range of cells, what default option can you choose?

Thick Box Border.

14. How do you clear all borders from around a cell or cells?

Highlight the cells and then choose the No Border option from the dropdown or the None border option in the Format Cells dialogue box.

15. How do you add background color to a cell?

Use Fill Color which can be most easily accessed from the Font section of the Home tab by clicking on the paint bucket that by default has a yellow line under it.

16. If you need to use a custom fill color or custom font color, how do you do this?

Click on the fill color or font color dropdown to bring up the colors dropdown menu. At the bottom of the menu click on the More Colors option to bring up the Colors dialogue box. Go to the Custom tab and provide your RGB or HSL values.

17. Name three ways to adjust the width of a column.

Right-click on the column and choose Column Width from the dropdown menu and then input a value. Place your cursor to the right side of the column and then left-click and hold while dragging the column to the desired width. Or place your cursor on the right side of the column and double-left click to get the column to auto-adjust to the contents in the column.

18. How can you adjust all of your column widths at once?

Select all cells in the worksheet and then either double-left click on any column to get the columns to adjust to their contents or left-click and drag on one column's border line to change all column widths to the same new column width. If you need a specific column width you can also select all cells in the worksheet and then right-click on a column and choose Column Width to specify the needed column width.

19. How do you select all cells in a worksheet?

Click in the top left corner between the label for Column A and Row 1. Or use Ctrl + A.

20. Name three ways to adjust the height of a row.

Right-click on the row and choose Row Height from the dropdown menu and then input a value. Place your cursor at the bottom of the row and then left-click and hold while dragging the row to the desired height. Or place your cursor on the bottom of the row and double-left click to get the row to auto-adjust to the contents in the column.

21. How can you adjust all of your row heights at once?

Select all cells in the worksheet and then either double-left click on any row to get the rows to adjust to their contents or left-click and drag on any row border line to change all row heights to the same new row height. If you need a specific row height you can also select all cells in the worksheet and then right-click on a row and choose Row Height to specify the needed row height.

22. How do you get text to wrap to the next line?

Use Wrap Text which is available under the Alignment section of the Home tab. It's also available by right-clicking, choosing Format Cells, going to the Alignment tab, and selecting the Wrap Text option.

23. Name three ways you can apply currency formatting to a cell or range of cells.

Click on the $ sign in the Number section of the Home tab. Go to the Number section of the Home tab and choose Accounting or Currency from the dropdown menu. Right-click and choose Format Cells from the dropdown menu and then go to the Number tab and choose either Currency or Accounting from there.

24. Name two ways you can apply date formatting to a cell or range of cells.

Go to the Number section of the Home tab and choose the Short Date or Long Date option from the dropdown menu. Or right-click, choose Format Cells from the dropdown menu, go to the Number tab and choose Date for the category and then a date format from one of the available samples.

25. What is one thing to be careful of when using dates in Excel?

You need to be aware that Excel will always assign a year to a date even if you don't. So if you type in Jan-1, Excel will make that date into January 1st of the current year.

26. Name two ways you can change the font used in a cell or range of cells.

Go to the Font section of the Home tab and choose a different font from the font dropdown box. Right click, choose Format Cells from the dropdown menu, go to the Font tab, and choose your Font from the available list of fonts.

27. Name four ways to change the size of the font used in a cell or range of cells.

Go to the Font section of the Home tab and choose a different font size from the font size dropdown menu. Go to the Font section of the Home tab and type in a new font size where the current font size is displayed. Go to the Font section of the Home tab and use the Increase Font Size and Decrease Font Size options. Right-click, choose Format Cells, go to the Font tab and choose a new font size from the listed values or type in a new value.

28. How do you change the color of the text in a cell or range of cells?

Go to the Font section of the Home tab and click on the Font Color dropdown, which is the A with a red line under it by default, and then choose the color you want from the listed options or by clicking on More Colors. Or you can right-click, choose to Format Cells, go to the Font tab, and click on the dropdown menu under Color and choose a color from there.

29. If you've placed a dark fill color into a cell, what font color might you want to use?

White or another light color that will show over a dark color.

30. What does Merge & Center do?

It merges multiple cells into one cell and centers any text that was in the top left cell of the range across the newly-created single cell.

31. When might you want to use Merge & Center?

When creating a table of data where you want a single cell that runs across the top that labels a range of cells below that.

32. How do you Merge & Center a range of cells?

Highlight the cells you want to merge, go to the Alignment section of the Home tab and choose Merge & Center. You can also highlight the cells, right-click, choose Format Cells from the dropdown menu, go to the Alignment tab, and then choose Merge Cells from there. With this option you'll have to center the text separately.

33. If you want to format a range of cells as a number with four decimal places, how would you do that?

Highlight the cells and then go to the Number section of the Home tab and choose the Number option from the dropdown menu. This will create a number with two decimal places. Next, click on the Increase Decimal option twice to add two more decimal places. Or you can highlight the cells, right-click, choose Format Cells, go to the Number tab, choose Number on the left-hand side, and then in the middle specify the number of decimal places you need.

34. How do you format a number as a percentage?

You can click on the percent sign in the Number section of the Home tab or you can right-click, choose Format Cells, go to the Number tab, and choose Percentage from there.

35. If you have the number .10 what is that as a percentage?

10%

36. What does the Format Painter allow you to do?

It allows you to copy the formatting from one cell or a range of cells to another cell or range of cells.

37. How do you use the Format Painter?

Click on the selection that has the formatting you want, then click on the Format Painter tool under the Clipboard section of the Home tab, then highlight the cell or cells where you want to apply that formatting.

38. What would happen if you click on the Format Painter tool and then try to use the arrow keys to navigate to the cell where you want to apply that formatting?

You'd end up applying that formatting to the first cell you arrow to.

39. How can you apply formatting to multiple cells that are not touching without having to go through the whole Format Painter process each time?

Click on the selection that has the formatting you want, *double-click* on the Format Painter tool, and then click on all of the cells you want to have that formatting before clicking on the Format Painter tool again to turn it off.

MANIPULATING YOUR DATA
QUIZ ANSWERS

1. What does Sorting do?

It allows you to take a range of cells and sort them based upon criteria you specify. For example, by date and then customer name and then amount spent.

2. Do you need to have a header row to sort data?

No.

3. If your data does have a header row, what do you need to make sure you do when you are telling Excel how to sort your data?

Make sure "my data has headers" is selected in the top right corner of the Sort dialogue box.

4. What will happen if your data has a header row but Excel doesn't know that?

Excel will sort the header row as if it's any other row of data.

5. Should you include a summary row in your sort?

No. Because Excel will treat that summary row as any other row of data and will sort it that way.

6. Name three ways to sort a range of data.

Select the cells you want to sort, go to the Editing section of the Home tab, click on the Sort & Filter dropdown, and choose Custom Sort. You can also go to the Data tab and click on the Sort option there. Or you can right-click and choose Sort and then Custom Sort from the dropdown menu.

7. If the sort options that you see are Column A, Column B, Column C, etc. what does this mean?

That Excel doesn't think that your data has a header row.

8. What order should you list your sort criteria in?

From the first one you want used to the last one you want used. So if you want to sort by date and then name, be sure to list date as your first sort criteria and name second.

9. If you want to sort text in an alphabetical order, which sort options should you choose?

Values and A to Z.

10. If you want to sort numbers from largest to smallest, which sort options should you choose?

Values and Largest to Smallest.

11. If you have a range that contains days of the week or months of the year, what sort options should you choose?

Values, Custom List, and then the list that corresponds to how you've written the days of the week or months of the year.

12. If you added a sort level that you don't need, how do you remove it?

Click on that level and then choose Delete Level.

13. How do you change the order in which your data will be sorted when you have multiple sort criteria listed?

Click on a level you want to move and then use the up and down arrows at the top of the Sort dialogue box to move your sort criteria into the desired order.

14. What are some issues to be aware of when sorting?

Be sure that you've selected all related data before you sort. If you only select one column of data and sort it, the data in other columns will not sort and that can lead to a mismatch in your data entries. (Another reason to always keep your raw data stored in one location and to manipulate that data elsewhere.)

That if you have a header column and don't tell Excel that it's a header column it will be included in the sort just like any other row. Same with any summary row.

15. What should you do if you sort data and realize you made a mistake?

Ctrl + Z to Undo the sort and try again.

16. What does filtering do?

It allows you to take a set of data and apply filters to that data so that only certain results are displayed. The underlying data remains in the same order as before.

17. How do you turn on filtering?

Click into a cell in the header row of your data and then go to the Editing section of the Home tab, click on the arrow next to Sort & Filter, and choose Filter.

18. If you add a new column of data, will filtering extend to that new column?

No. You will need to turn off filtering and then turn it back on to include the new column.

19. How will you know when you have filtering turned on?

You'll see small gray arrows in the bottom right corner of the header row for each column that has filtering available.

20. Once you've turned on filtering, how do you filter a specific column?

Click on the gray arrow in the header row for that column and then choose your filter criteria.

21. In recent versions of Excel, what options do you have for filtering data?

You can specify text, you can click on the box to select specific entries, you can use text or number filters, and you can filter by cell or font color.

22. Using filtering, if you just want to see two or three specific entries in a column but have a large number of different values that are possible in that column, what's a quick trick to do that?

Click on the Select All option to unselect all of the entries and then just click on the two or three entries you want to see.

23. Using filtering, if you want to see all of the entries that contain the word "USA", how would you do that?

Use the Search option and type in USA.

24. Using filtering, if you want to see all of the entries that have red text, how would you do that?

Use the Filter by Color option, choose Filter by Font Color, and then click on the red option.

25. Using filtering, if you want to see all of the entries with a numerical value greater than 100, how would you do that?

Use the Number Filters option, choose Greater Than, and then specify 100 as your value.

26. How can you tell when your worksheet values have already been filtered?
The row numbers in your worksheet will be colored blue and you'll see that the row numbers skip values.

27. How can you tell which columns have filtering in place?
The gray arrow will turn into a funnel.

28. How do you remove filtering from a specific column?
Click on the funnel and choose Clear Filter from [Column Name].

29. How do you remove filtering from all columns in a worksheet?
Go to the Editing section of the Home tab, click on Sort & Filter, and then choose Clear.

30. How do you turn off filtering?
Go to the Editing section of the Home tab, click on Sort & Filter, and click on Filter.

31. How do you tell Excel that you want to use a function?
Start your entry with an = sign.

32. What is the function you can use to sum a range of values?
SUM

33. What is the function you can use to multiply a range of values?
PRODUCT

34. Is there a function for subtracting values?
No.

35. Is there a function for dividing values?
No.

36. What is the symbol you can use to add two values?
The + symbol.

37. What is the symbol you can use to multiply two values?
The * symbol.

38. What is the symbol you can use to subtract two values?
The - symbol.

39. What is the symbol you can use to divide two values?
The / symbol

40. What cells am I referencing if I write =SUM(A1:B3)?
Cells A1, B1, A2, B2, A3, and B3

41. What cells am I referencing if I write =SUM(A1,B3)?
Cells A1 and B3

42. What cells am I referencing if I write =SUM(A:B)?
All the cells in Columns A and B

43. What cells am I referencing if I write =SUM(1:3)?
All the cells in Rows 1, 2, and 3

44. If you just want to know what the sum of a range of cells is but don't need to record that value anywhere, what is one option you have for seeing that sum?

You can simply select the cells and then look in the bottom right corner of the Excel worksheet where it shows the SUM for the selected cells.

45. How can you see what cells are being used in a formula?

Double-click into the cell where the formula is and Excel will highlight all of the cells being used in the formula in a color that matches the cell reference within the formula that you're reviewing.

46. What does AutoSum do?

It allows you to sum a range of values by clicking in the cell at the end of that range of values and choosing the AutoSum option. Excel will then write the sum formula for you.

47. Where can you find the AutoSum option?

In the Editing section of the Home tab.

48. What is one thing to be careful about when using AutoSum?

If there are gaps in the range of values you want to sum, the AutoSum function will not sum the entire range of values, but will instead stop at the first gap in your data.

49. If you want to subtract the values in Cells B1, C1, and D1 from the value in Cell A1, what's the best way to do that?

Use the formula =A1-SUM(B1:D1)

(Writing =A1-B1-C1-D1 would also work, but is not the best way to do it.)

50. How can you get Excel to help you write your formulas?

Once you start a function or formula, Excel will populate any cells that you highlight into the function or formula. So you can type =SUM(and then go highlight the range of values you want to sum and Excel will translate those highlight cells into cell notation for you. This is especially helpful when you're using cell references across worksheets.

51. Is it possible to use Excel to conduct complex calculations in one cell?

Yes, but be careful about where you place your parens to make sure that the calculations are performed in the correct order.

52. How do you find a function that can do what you want to do?

Go to the Formulas tab and click on Insert Function to bring up the Insert Function dialogue box. You can then search in the "search for a function" box and then click on the functions Excel lists to see a description of what each one does and how to write it.

53. What does it mean that formulas in Excel are relative?

It means that when you copy a formula to a new cell it will adjust all of the cell references based on how far the formula was moved. So A1+B1 becomes C1+D1 if that formula is copied over two columns and becomes A3+B3 if it's copied down two rows.

54. Why is it good that formulas in Excel are relative?

Because this allows you to write a formula once and then copy it to a large number of cells without having to rewrite it each time. For example, if you're calculating amount owed from your customers based upon how many units of your product they bought you can write a formula that multiplies units times price and then just copy that down all the customer rows. As long as units and price are in the same relative location for each customer, you only have to write the formula that one time.

55. What if you want to keep a reference fixed when you copy a formula? For example, Cell A1 includes the unit price and you want that fixed no matter where you copy the formula to?

Then use the $ sign to fix your cell reference. If you want to always be referencing Cell A1 than the formula should use A1.

56. What if you just want to move a formula but you don't want any of the cell references to change. How would you do that?

Then cut that formula (Ctrl + X) instead of copying the formula (Ctrl + C). You can also click into the cell, copy the text of the formula, go to the new location, and paste the text in that way.

PRINTING
QUIZ ANSWERS

1. What is the control shortcut for printing?
Ctrl + P

2. How else can you access the print option?
Go to the File tab and select Print.

3. If you're ready to print and don't need to make any changes, what button do you click on to print?
The printer icon labeled print.

4. If you want to print on both sides of the page, which option should you change?
The one that by default is labeled print one sided.

5. When is it best to use print on both sides long-edge versus print on both sides short-edge?
It's best to print on both sides long-edge when your document has a portrait orientation and to use print on both sides short-edge when your document has a landscape orientation.

6. What does it mean to print a document collated versus uncollated?

This only matters when there are multiple pages to the document and you're printing more than one copy. If you print collated all pages for each copy will print at once. If you print uncollated the first page will print for as many copies as you specified and then the second page will print and so on.

7. What does Print Selection do?

It prints only the cells you've highlighted in your Excel workbook. (This can mean that you print across worksheets if you happened to have multiple worksheets selected when you highlighted your cells.)

8. What does Print Active Sheets do?

It prints all of the worksheets that you've selected. You can select multiple worksheets by using the Ctrl key as you click on each one.

9. What does Print Entire Workbook do?

It prints all worksheets in your Excel file.

10. What does Print Selected Pages do?

It allows you to only print certain pages from your selected worksheet(s). You can use the Print Preview to see what information is available on each page.

11. How do you change the printer you're using to print?

Select a new printer from the dropdown menu under Printer at the top of the screen.

12. How do you specify the number of copies to print?

Change the number where it says Copies at the top of the screen. You can either use the arrows or type in a new value.

13. What is the difference between portrait orientation and landscape orientation?

Portrait orientation has the longer edge of the page along the side and the shorter edge at the top, like most books. Landscape orientation has the long edge at the top and the short edge on the side, like many landscape paintings or PowerPoint presentations.

14. How do you choose what type of paper to print on?

Change the dropdown that by default says Letter to the type of paper you need to print on.

15. What should you be careful about when selecting the type of paper to print on?

Make sure that type of paper is actually available to you to print on.

16. What does the margins setting let you do?

Change the amount of white space that's left available around the edges of the page.

17. What does scaling let you do?

Reduce the overall size of your information so that it fits onto one page or so that all rows or columns fit on one page.

18. What should you be careful about when using page scaling?

That you don't make the information so small that it's no longer legible.

19. What's one trick for working with scaling if the data isn't going to fit well on the page?

Change your document orientation to landscape so that more columns can fit on the page without reducing the size of the font as much.

20. Where can you go to scale your document?

If you just want to fit everything on one page or all columns or rows on one page those options are available on the main print screen under the dropdown that by default says No Scaling. But if you want to scale across a specified number of pages, then you can click on Page Setup and go to the Page tab and then specify your number of pages wide and tall.

21. Where can you go to center your print output horizontally and/or vertically on the page?

Click on Page Setup and then go to the Margins tab and click the option you want.

22. What does setting a Print Area on a document do?

It limits the area of that document that will be printed to just the selected range of cells.

23. When is setting the Print Area useful?

When you have a number of calculations or notes on a worksheet, but only ever want to print a small section of that worksheet.

24. What are the dangers of using Print Area?

If you add more information to the worksheet but forget that you've set a print area, you may not understand why the new data isn't printing.

25. What's the best way to set the Print Area?

While you're in the active worksheet, highlight the cells you want to print, go to the Page Layout tab, and click on the Print Area dropdown, and choose Set Print Area from there.

26. What does Print Titles allow you to do?

It allows you to specify a row or rows and a column or columns that will print on every single page of your document. This is great when you have a large set of data that can't be printed on one page and need a header row or column with identifiers visible on each page.

27. How do you set Print Titles?

While in your active worksheet go to the Page Layout tab and click on Print Titles. This will bring up the Sheet tab of the Page Setup dialogue box. Click in the box for rows to repeat at the top and then select the rows you want to have repeat from your worksheet. Next, click on the box for columns to repeat at left and select the columns you want to repeat.

28. What should you be careful of when using Print Titles?

If you tell Excel to repeat too many rows at the top or too many columns on the side you can end up just printing those rows and columns over and over again without printing the rest of the data in the worksheet.

CONCLUSION QUIZ ANSWERS

1. Name three ways to find more information if you get stuck.

Click on the ? mark in the top right corner of your Excel workbook and search for information on the topic. Click on the Tell Me More option available under certain menu items, such as Format Painter. Do an internet search on your topic and look for the www.support.office.com search result.

2. What else can you do if you get stuck?

Search for forums where someone else has already asked your question. Or email me at mlhumphreywriter@gmail.com.

BONUS: EXERCISES

EXERCISE 1

Recreate the following image where the total value in Column E is calculated by multiplying the units times the price for each customer.

	A	B	C	D	E
1	Date	Customer Name	Units	Price	Total
2	1/1/2018	Bob Jones	10	$2.50	$25.00
3	3/4/2018	Albert Cross	15	$2.50	$37.50
4	5/1/2018	Bob Jones	10	$2.50	$25.00
5	6/1/2018	Albert Cross	20	$2.50	$50.00
6					

EXERCISE 2

Recreate the following image where the values in Cells I5 and K5 sum the values in the three rows above those cells:

	H	I	J	K	L
1		Cash	Category	CC	
2		$0.00	Gas	$59.73	
3		$13.02	Misc	$0.00	
4		$0.00	Groceries	$94.21	
5		$13.02	TOTAL	$153.94	
6					

EXERCISE 3

Recreate the following image making sure to use AutoComplete to populate the days of the week and an addition formula to populate the dates in Rows 3 through 8. Also, Column J should be the total of the values in Columns C through I for each row.

	A	B	C	D	E	F	G	H	I	J
1			Monday	Tuesday	Wednesda	Thursday	Friday	Saturday	Sunday	
2	7/3/2017	7/9/2017	0.25	1.5	2.5	3.5	0.5	0	1	9.25
3	7/10/2017	7/16/2017								0
4	7/17/2017	7/23/2017								0
5	7/24/2017	7/30/2017								0
6	7/31/2017	8/6/2017								0
7	8/7/2017	8/13/2017								0
8	8/14/2017	8/20/2017								0
9										

EXERCISE 4

Recreate the following image where the values in Column E are the product of the values in Columns C and D for each row, the values in Column F is the value in Column B divided by Cell B3 for each row, and the values in Column G are the value in Column E times the value in Column F for each row.

	A	B	C	D	E	F	G
1							
2		Amazon Unit Sales	List Price	Payout	Net Per Sale	% Book 1 to This Book	Value of New Customer
3	Book 1	500	$0.99	35%	$0.35	100%	$0.35
4	Book 2	250	$3.99	70%	$2.79	50%	$1.40
5	Book 3	125	$4.99	70%	$3.49	25%	$0.87
6	Book 4	100	$4.99	70%	$3.49	20%	$0.70
7	Book 5	75	$5.99	70%	$4.19	15%	$0.63
8							$3.94

EXERCISE 5

Recreate the following image where the values in Cells C3 through H7 are calculated values using a formula copies from Cell C3 that uses the $ sign to keep the references to Column B and Row 2 fixed. The formula in Cell C3 multiplies the value in Cell C2 by the value in B3.

	A	B	C	D	E	F	G	H
1		Weekly			Hours Worked			
2			10	20	30	40	50	60
3		$8.50	$85.00	$170.00	$255.00	$340.00	$425.00	$510.00
4	Wages	$9.00	$90.00	$180.00	$270.00	$360.00	$450.00	$540.00
5		$9.50	$95.00	$190.00	$285.00	$380.00	$475.00	$570.00
6		$10.00	$100.00	$200.00	$300.00	$400.00	$500.00	$600.00
7		$10.50	$105.00	$210.00	$315.00	$420.00	$525.00	$630.00
8								

Quiz 3

BONUS:
EXERCISE ANSWERS

For
Quiz
#3

Exercise
1 & 2
multipl Addition sub
Dividing Compare

EXERCISE 1

Recreate the following image where the total value in Column E is calculated by multiplying the units times the price for each customer.

	A	B	C	D	E
1	Date	Customer Name	Units	Price	Total
2	1/1/2018	Bob Jones	10	$2.50	$25.00
3	3/4/2018	Albert Cross	15	$2.50	$37.50
4	5/1/2018	Bob Jones	10	$2.50	$25.00
5	6/1/2018	Albert Cross	20	$2.50	$50.00
6					

1. Enter "Date", "Customer Name", "Units", "Price" and "Total" in Cells A1 through E1 respectively.

2. Enter "1/1", "3/4", "5/1" and "6/1 in Cells A2 through A5 respectively. Format as Short Date.

3. Enter "Bob Jones", "Albert Cross", "Bob Jones", and "Albert Cross" into Cells B2 through B5 respectively.

4. Enter "10", "15", "10", and "20" into Cells C2 through C5 respectively.

5. Enter $2.50 into Cell D2 and format as Currency. Copy down to Cells D3 through D5.

6. Add the formula =C2*D2 to Cell E2 and then copy it down to Cells E3 through E5.

7. Highlight the columns and double-left click on the side of Column B to autosize the column width to the contents.

8. Italicize the dates in Column A.

9. Underline the column headers in Row 1.

10. Place a basic border (All Borders) around Cells A1 through E5.

11. Place a darker outer border (Thick Box Border) around Cells A1 through E5.

EXERCISE 2

Recreate the following image where the values in Cells I5 and K5 sum the values in the three rows above those cells:

	H	I	J	K	L
1		**Cash**	**Category**	**CC**	
2		$0.00	**Gas**	$59.73	
3		$13.02	**Misc**	$0.00	
4		$0.00	**Groceries**	$94.21	
5		**$13.02**	**TOTAL**	**$153.94**	
6					

1. In Cells I1 through I3 type "Cash", "Category", and "CC" respectively.

2. In Cells J2 through J5 type "Gas", "Misc", "Groceries", and "TOTAL" respectively.

3. In Cells I2 through I4 type "0", "13.02", and "0" respectively.

4. In Cells K2 through K4 type "59.73", "0", and "94.21" respectively.

5. In Cell I5 add the formula =SUM(I2:I4).

6. In Cell K5 add the formula =SUM(K2:K4).

7. Bold the values in Cells I1 through K1 and Cells J2 through J5, and in Cells I5 and K5.

8. Format Cells I2 through I5 and K2 through K5 as Currency.

9. Add a fill color to Cells I1 through K1 and J2 through J5.

10. Add a basic border (All Borders) around all of the cells.

11. Center align all of the cells.

EXERCISE 3

Recreate the following image making sure to use AutoComplete to populate the days of the week and an addition formula to populate the dates in Rows 3 through 8. Also, Column J should be the total of the values in Columns C through I for each row.

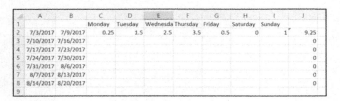

▲	A	B	C	D	E	F	G	H	I	J
1			Monday	Tuesday	Wednesda	Thursday	Friday	Saturday	Sunday	
2	7/3/2017	7/9/2017	0.25	1.5	2.5	3.5	0.5	0	1	9.25
3	7/10/2017	7/16/2017								0
4	7/17/2017	7/23/2017								0
5	7/24/2017	7/30/2017								0
6	7/31/2017	8/6/2017								0
7	8/7/2017	8/13/2017								0
8	8/14/2017	8/20/2017								0
9										

1. Type "Monday" into Cell C1 and then click and drag from the bottom right corner of the cell over to Cell I1 to populate the rest of the days of the week.

2. Type "7/3/17" and "7/9/17" into Cells A2 and B2 respectively.

3. In Cell A3 add the formula =A2+7.

4. Copy the formula from Cell A3 to Cells A3 through B8. Adjust Column B's width so that all dates are visible.

5. In Cells C2 through I2 add the values "0.25", "1.5", "2.5", "3.5.", "0.5", "0", and "1" respectively.

6. In Cell J2 add the formula =SUM(C2:I2). (You could use AutoSum here as well.)

7. Copy the formula from J2 to Cells J3 through J8.

EXERCISE 4

Recreate the following image where the values in Column E are the product of the values in Columns C and D for each row, the values in Column F is the value in Column B divided by Cell B3 for each row, and the values in Column G are the value in Column E times the value in Column F for each row.

	A	B	C	D	E	F	G
1							
2		Amazon Unit Sales	List Price	Payout	Net Per Sale	% Book 1 to This Book	Value of New Customer
3	Book 1	500	$0.99	35%	$0.35	100%	$0.35
4	Book 2	250	$3.99	70%	$2.79	50%	$1.40
5	Book 3	125	$4.99	70%	$3.49	25%	$0.87
6	Book 4	100	$4.99	70%	$3.49	20%	$0.70
7	Book 5	75	$5.99	70%	$4.19	15%	$0.63
8							$3.94

1. In Cells B2 through G2 add the text "Amazon Unit Sales", "List Price", "Payout", "Net Per Sale", "% Book 1 to This Book", and "Value of New Customer" respectively.

2. In Cells A3 through A7 add "Book 1", "Book 2", "Book3", "Book4" and "Book 5". (You can just add Book 1 and Book 2 and then highlight both cells and click and drag from the bottom right corner of Cell A4 to populate the rest of the values.)

3. Bold the entries in Cells B2 through G2 and A3 through A7. Wrap text for Cells B2 through G2.

4. In Cells B3 through B7 add the values "500", "250", "125", "100" and "75" respectively.

5. In Cells C3 through C7 add the values "0.99", "3.99", "4.99", "4.99", and "5.99" respectively. Format as Currency.

6. In Cells D3 through D4 add the values ".35" and ".7", respectively. Format as a Percentage and then copy the value from Cell D4 to Cells D5 through D7.

7. In Cell E3 add the formula =C3*D3.

8. Copy the value in Cell E3 to Cells E4 through E7.

9. In Cell F3 add the formula =B3/B3. Copy the formula from Cell F3 to Cells F4 through F7 and format Cells F3 through F7 as a percentage.

10. In Cell G3 add the formula =E3*F3.

11. Copy the value from G3 to G4 through G7.

12. In Cell G8 use AutoSum to sum the values in Cells G3 through G7. Bold the result. (You can also just use a SUM function =SUM(G3:G7).)

13. Place a basic border (All Borders) around Cells B3 through G7.

EXERCISE 5

Recreate the following image where the values in Cells C3 through H7 are calculated values using a formula copies from Cell C3 that uses the $ sign to keep the references to Column B and Row 2 fixed. The formula in Cell C3 multiplies the value in Cell C2 by the value in B3.

	A	B	C	D	E	F	G	H
1		Weekly			Hours Worked			
2			10	20	30	40	50	60
3		$8.50	$85.00	$170.00	$255.00	$340.00	$425.00	$510.00
4	Wages	$9.00	$90.00	$180.00	$270.00	$360.00	$450.00	$540.00
5		$9.50	$95.00	$190.00	$285.00	$380.00	$475.00	$570.00
6		$10.00	$100.00	$200.00	$300.00	$400.00	$500.00	$600.00
7		$10.50	$105.00	$210.00	$315.00	$420.00	$525.00	$630.00
8								

1. In Cell B1 type "Weekly" and bold it.

2. In Cell C1 type "Hours Worked" and bold it.

3. Select Cells C1 through H1 and Merge & Center.

4. Add fill color to the newly merged cell that spans Cells C1 through H1.

5. In Cell A3 type "Wages" and bold it.

6. Select Cells A3 through A7 and Merge and Center.

7. Add fill color to the newly merged cell that spans Cells A3 through A7.

8. Change the orientation of the text that spans Cells A3 through A7 to Rotate Text Up and adjust the column width to fit the text. Middle Align the text in the cell.

9. In Cells B3 through B7 add the values "8.50", "9.00", "9.50", "10.00", and "10.50", respectively. (This could also be done with a mathematical formula as well where you input 8.50 and then use =B3+.5 in the next cell and copy that formula down the rest of the way.)

10. In Cells C2 through H2 add the values "10", "20", "30", "40", "50", and "60" respectively. (This could also be done with a mathematical formula where you type 10 into Cells C2 and then =C2+10 into D2 and copy that formula to the rest of the cells.)

11. Add fill color to Cells B3 through B7 and C2 through H2.

12. In Cell C3 type the following formula: =C$2*$B3.

13. Copy the formula from Cell C3 to cells C3 through H7.

14. Add All Borders around Cells C1 through H7 and around Cells A3 through B7.

15. Format Cells B3 through H7 as Currency.

INDEX OF QUIZZES

ABOUT THE AUTHOR

M.L. Humphrey is a former stockbroker with a degree in Economics from Stanford and an MBA from Wharton who has spent close to twenty years as a regulator and consultant in the financial services industry.

You can reach M.L. at mlhumphreywriter@gmail.com or at mlhumphrey.com.

Made in the USA
Monee, IL
21 November 2019

17197401R00059